21st
Century
Skills Library

REAL WORLD MATH: GEOGRAPHY

VOLCANOES

BY JOHN NESTOR

CHERRY LAKE
Publishing

Published in the United States of America by
Cherry Lake Publishing, Ann Arbor, Michigan
www.cherrylakepublishing.com

Content Adviser
Andrew Dombard, Associate Professor, Department of Earth and Environmental
Sciences, University of Illinois at Chicago
Math Adviser: Tonya Walker, MA, Boston University

Credits
Photos: Cover and page 1, ©juliengrondin, used under license from Shutterstock, Inc.;
page 4, ©Sam Dcruz, used under license from Shutterstock, Inc.; page 7, ©Peder
Digre, used under license from Shutterstock, Inc.; page 8, ©JUPITERIMAGES/
Brand X/Alamy; page 10, ©Thumeau/Dreamstime.com; page 12, ©Juliengrondin/
Dreamstime.com; pages 14 and 23, ©Jose Gil, used under license from Shutterstock,
Inc.; page 15, ©Pichugin Dmitry, used under license from Shutterstock, Inc.; page 17,
©Jimsphotos/Dreamstime.com; page 18, ©ARCTIC IMAGES/Alamy; page 20,
©Ironrodart/Dreamstime.com; page 24, ©imagebroker/Alamy; page 26, ©Kevin
Schafer/Alamy; page 27, ©Boztank/Dreamstime.com

Library of Congress Cataloging-in-Publication Data
Nestor, John.
  Volcanoes / by John Nestor.
      p. cm.—(Real world math: geography)
  Includes index.
  ISBN-13: 978-1-60279-491-7
  ISBN-10: 1-60279-491-X
  1. Volcanoes—Juvenile literature. I. Title.
II. Series.
  QE521.3.N47 2010
  551.21—dc22   2008048301

Cherry Lake Publishing would like to acknowledge
the work of The Partnership for 21st Century Skills.
Please visit *www.21stcenturyskills.org* for more information.

TABLE OF CONTENTS

CHAPTER ONE
WHAT ARE VOLCANOES?

Have you ever climbed a mountain? You have probably seen one. Perhaps it was a small nearby mountain. Or maybe it was the Rocky Mountains in the United States, or the Andes in South America, or the Alps in Europe! If you have seen a mountain, then you know what a volcano looks like.

An erupting volcano is an amazing sight.

Volcanoes are mountains that rise over time, growing as they erupt. When a volcano erupts, **magma** comes up from inside the earth. Magma is a **molten**, or melted, rock under Earth's surface. Magma pours out onto Earth's surface as **lava**. (Lava is what magma is called after it flows out of a volcano.)

LEARNING & INNOVATION SKILLS

People around the world live near volcanoes. Almost 20 million people live in and around Mexico City, near an **active** volcano. Popocatépetl is less than 45 miles (72 kilometers) from Mexico City, the capital of Mexico. It erupted in 1994 and again in 1996.

Living near a volcano has its benefits. The soil is usually rich for farming. Thermal energy from volcanoes can help produce electric power. Volcanoes often bring tourism, which employs local workers.

But if a volcano erupts, it can cause death and destroy homes. Volcanic activity also produces clouds of ash and poisonous gases. Would you live near a volcano? Why or why not?

A volcanic eruption can look like a huge bomb going off. Ash and cinders fly into the air. Lava gushes out like a fiery river over the side of the volcano.

That's what happened at 8:32 A.M. on May 18, 1980. Mount Saint Helens, a part of the Cascade Range in Washington State, erupted. The volcano blasted 230 square miles (596 square kilometers) of forest. Almost 60 people lost their lives. Large numbers of animals, birds, and fish were killed. There was more than $1 billion of damage.

Above Mount Saint Helens, a column of volcanic ash rose up into the sky. Ash fell in 11 states. A series of volcanic mudslides reached as far as the Columbia River. That's nearly 50 miles (80 km) south of the eruption.

REAL WORLD MATH CHALLENGE

The 1980 Mount Saint Helens volcano blew bits of rock at a speed of 250 miles per hour. We know 1 mile equals about 1.6 kilometers. **How many kilometers per hour did the rocks move through the air?**

(Turn to page 29 for the answer)

The eruption left Mount Saint Helens with a deep hole. That **crater** was nearly 1 mile (1.6 km) wide and 2,500 feet (762 m) deep. It was one of the greatest volcanic explosions on record in North America.

Mount Saint Helens remains active.

CHAPTER TWO
MAGMA, EXPLOSIONS, ASH

Volcanoes come in many different shapes and sizes.
Some erupt in short bursts and then go silent for many years.
Others show some volcanic activity every day for years at a
time. Some volcanoes are on land. Others are at the bottom of
the ocean.

Sea lions bask on the island of Española.
Volcanic activity created the island.

There are many different kinds of volcanic eruptions. The way a volcano erupts determines how the volcano is classified. It can be difficult to classify a volcano, but here are four main kinds of volcanoes.

The first kind of volcano is formed when thin, fluid lava flows rapidly from a volcano over time. The lava does not explode high into the sky. These volcanoes have low, sloping sides. These broad, rounded volcanoes are called **shield volcanoes**. These are some of the largest volcanoes on Earth. Hawaii's and Iceland's volcanoes are examples of shield volcanoes.

REAL WORLD MATH CHALLENGE

Ecuador's Galápagos Islands are young in geologic terms. But volcanic activity on the seafloor helped form one of the islands, Española, 3 to 5 million years ago! A recent study shows that the Galápagos Islands region is one of the world's most active volcanic areas. About 50 eruptions have taken place in the last 500 years. **On average, how often is there a volcanic eruption on the Galápagos Islands?**

(Turn to page 29 for the answer)

The second kind of volcano forms when the magma is slightly thicker. The magma traps gases. The pressure continues to build until ash and rock finally explode through the volcano's opening, or **vent**. The cinders collect close to the vent to build a **cinder cone**. Mexico's Paricutín is a cinder cone. It's about 10,400 feet (3,170 m) high. When it first erupted in 1943, lava buried the town.

The third kind of volcano is formed by several eruptions. After a fluid magma flows, a thicker magma erupts. The layers build up to form **stratovolcanoes**. These volcanoes are made of erupted cinders and ash with occasional lava flows. Mount Fuji is an example of a stratovolcano. At 12,388 feet (3,776 m), it is Japan's tallest mountain.

The fourth kind of volcano can be the most spectacular. **Caldera volcanoes** are formed when enormous

Stratovolcanoes, such as Mount Fuji in Japan, can be very tall.

explosions cause the central part of the volcano to collapse. This causes a huge depression called a caldera. Sometimes these calderas fill with water to form lakes. Crater Lake in Oregon is a caldera that filled with water. The caldera was formed more than 6,000 years ago.

LIFE & CAREER SKILLS

Are you interested in learning more about volcanoes? Then why not study volcanology? A volcanologist is a person who studies volcanoes and volcanic events. Volcanologists observe eruptions and volcanic activity. They collect valuable information in the field. They also work in offices, writing reports, or in labs, conducting experiments. Volcanologists also educate the public about volcanoes.

Most volcanologists have a strong background in one of the natural sciences. They also have great computer and math skills. Almost all volcanologists have a master of science or doctoral degree. There are many colleges and universities with excellent programs to prepare students for this exciting career.

CHAPTER THREE

DO THE MATH: GASES AND ROCKS

Duter eruption, gases and lava blast out through the volcano's vent. A vent can be located on the slope of a volcano or at its peak.

Sometimes lava shoots out of a vent with great force.

An eruption looks like boiling water spilling over the side of a pot. Some of the lava spills out of the vent. Hot lava can be as hot as 2,200 degrees Fahrenheit (1,204 degrees Celsius). It glows red to white as it flows.

21ST CENTURY CONTENT

Volcanoes produce a lot of harmful gases. These gases are one cause of global warming. However, they are not the only cause. Humans are also responsible for global warming. Part of our efforts to stop global warming will come from the study of volcanic emissions. But we also need to find ways to lower the amount of gases we create ourselves. The health of our planet depends on it.

What gases do volcanoes give off? The most important gas is water vapor. The second most important gas is carbon dioxide. Carbon dioxide is usually not dangerous. But when there is too much of it in a small space, this colorless, odorless gas can be deadly to people and animals. Carbon dioxide can also damage trees and plants.

Volcanic eruptions release other gases, including sulfur dioxide and hydrogen fluoride. These poisonous gases that make humans sick. They contribute to water and air pollution. These gases can even lower Earth's surface temperatures.

In addition to releasing a number of gases, volcanoes also make many different types of rocks. What kinds of rocks do volcanoes make?

Pumice is a kind of rock formed by rapidly cooling lava.

The gases given off by volcanoes can affect Earth's climate.

REAL WORLD MATH CHALLENGE

Assume that the temperature of a sample of molten lava is 2,200°F. **How much hotter is molten lava than boiling water?** (Hint: Water boils at 212°F.)

(Turn to page 29 for the answer)

Magma forms **igneous rock** when it cools. Granite is an example of igneous rock. Granite is formed from magma that never reaches Earth's surface. This hard rock is often used in building. Obsidian is a kind of glass that forms in nature. It is created in the same way as igneous rock. This dark volcanic glass forms when lava cools very quickly.

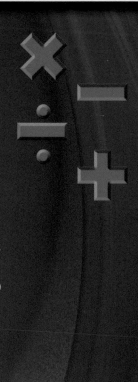

REAL WORLD MATH CHALLENGE

As magma reaches the surface, it gives off gases. It is difficult to measure the exact ratio of these gases. They change and react with one another as they rise. Scientists have come up with different figures for different volcanoes. Some experts studying Hawaiian volcanoes have found that magma heading toward the surface contains approximately 2% sulfur trioxide, less than 1% carbon monoxide, less than 1% hydrogen, less than 1% argon, 14% carbon dioxide, 6% sulfur dioxide, 5% nitrogen, and very small amounts of chlorine. The gases also contain a large percentage of water vapor.

Approximately what percentage of the gas mixture consists of water vapor?

(Turn to page 29 for the answer)

Obsidian is often used to create jewelry and other decorative objects.

Basalt is a very common volcanic rock. It is dark gray or black and shiny. The Hawaiian Islands are mostly made up of basalts. That's why some of their beaches have black sand.

We know that land around volcanoes has very rich soil. This is because it contains a lot of ash from previous volcano eruptions. As the ash breaks down over time, it releases nutrients such as iron, magnesium, and potassium into the soil. These nutrients are very important for growing plants. The ash also helps the soil hold water for a long time. This is especially useful in dry climates.

Volcanic soil helps farmers grow crops in Hawaii.

Because the soil is so fertile at the base of volcanoes, farming communities often develop there. The farmers know that there is always a chance of eruption, but the soil is so fertile that they choose to stay anyway.

Submarine volcanoes are known for **hydrothermal vents**. Hydrothermal vents are cracks in the ocean floor that shoot out hot water. They are found at very deep points in the ocean. The average depth of a hydrothermal vent is 7,000 feet (2134 m). The temperature of the water that shoots from these vents can reach 750°F (400°C)!

REAL WORLD MATH CHALLENGE

Nevado Coropuna is Peru's highest and largest volcano. It has more than six peaks scattered over an area that is about 13 miles long and 8 miles wide. **What is the area of this space?**

(Turn to page 29 for the answer)

Many unusual sea animals and plants live near hydrothermal vents. Since scientists first discovered the vents, more than 300 new species have been found living around them. There is no sunlight in such deep parts of the ocean. Because of this, the animals that live near hydrothermal vents are very different than the ones we see on land. Tubeworms, giant crabs, and sea anemones are just some of the strange creatures that live near hydrothermal vents.

There are volcanoes on land and under the water around the world. Where will you find the most volcanoes? Indonesia is the country with the most volcanoes. It has 76 historically active volcanoes!

LEARNING & INNOVATION SKILLS

Hawaii's Kilauea has been erupting since 1983. The local people must have understood the power of the mountain when they named it. The Hawaiian name *Kilauea* means "spewing" or "much spreading."

Each day, enough lava spills down the slopes of Kilauea to fill roughly 300 Olympic-size swimming pools. But you won't catch Michael Phelps going for gold in that pool. The temperature of Kilauea's lava is about 2,100°F (1,150°C)! At those temperatures, the lava buries, melts, or sets fire to anything it touches. Do you think that there is any way to protect buildings or wildlife in the path of this lava flow? Why or why not?

As lava pours into the water from Mount Kilauea, huge clouds of steam rise into the air.

The world's largest volcanic eruption on record took place at Indonesia's Mount Tambora in 1815. Tens of thousands of people were killed. The volcano also caused global warming the following year. Crops failed and people went hungry. Volcanic activity affects everyone in the world.

CHAPTER FIVE

VOLCANOES: FROM BIRTH TO ERUPTION

Huge, moving plates form Earth's crust. Some of Earth's volcanoes are located where these plates smash together. Other volcanoes are formed where the same plates move away from each other.

When Mount Pinatubo erupted in 1992, it created a gigantic crater.

Hot spots are places on Earth's surface where there is a lot of volcanic activity over time. Here, magma rises up and breaks through the plates.

Did you know that almost 80 percent of Earth's surface is volcanic? After Indonesia and Japan, the United States has the most historically active volcanoes. The United States has more than 100 volcanoes. Most of them are in Alaska and Hawaii. The other 48 states have about half of the country's volcanoes. Oregon and California have the most volcanoes of the 48 states.

LEARNING & INNOVATION SKILLS

Volcanic eruptions are often deadly. The 1991 eruption of Mount Pinatubo in the Philippines killed hundreds of people. And nearly 250,000 people had to leave their homes. What could a government do to help prevent loss of life and home in areas near active volcanoes?

The largest active volcano in the world is Mauna Loa in Hawaii. Mauna Loa is 13,677 feet (4,169 m) above sea level. It's not as tall as its neighbor, Mauna Kea. That's a large

dormant volcano, at 13,796 feet (4,205 m). It's not active now, but a dormant volcano could erupt again.

More than half of all active volcanoes in the world are part of the Ring of Fire. That's a region of frequent earthquakes and volcanic eruptions that encircles the Pacific Ocean. The Ring of Fire is also home to more earthquakes than anywhere else

The Arenal Volcano in Costa Rica is one of the many volcanoes located in the Ring of Fire.

Crater Lake is one of the most recognizable landmarks in Oregon.

on Earth. Why are there so many volcanoes and earthquakes in the Ring of Fire? Volcanoes and earthquakes are caused by Earth's plates moving against one another. The Ring of Fire is where the edges of many of these plates meet.

Do you live near the Ring of Fire, near Crater Lake, or in Hawaii? Maybe you live near a dormant volcano such as Canada's Mount Meager in British Columbia. Whether you live near a volcano or not, you probably live in an area affected and shaped by volcanic activity. That should help remind you that volcanoes are one of the greatest wonders of our natural world.

REAL WORLD MATH CHALLENGE

Indonesia rests within the Pacific Ring of Fire. In 1815, a volcanic mountain in Indonesia called Mount Tambora erupted. The aftermath was devastating. Mount Tambora was approximately 13,000 feet high before the eruption. After the eruption, Tambora only reached a height of approximately 9,354 feet. **By how much did the force of the eruption reduce the height of Mount Tambora?**

(Turn to page 29 for the answer)

REAL WORLD MATH CHALLENGE ANSWERS

Chapter One

Page 6

The rocks moved through the air at a speed of 400 kilometers per hour.
1 mile = 1.6 kilometers
250 x 1.6 kilometers =
400 kilometers

Chapter Two

Page 9

On average, there is an eruption on the Galápagos Islands every 10 years.
500 years ÷ 50 eruptions = 10 years

Chapter Three

Page 15

The temperature of the lava is 1,988°F hotter than boiling water.
2,200°F – 212°F = 1,988°F

Page 16

Water vapor makes up about 70% of the gas mixture.
2% + 1% + 1% + 1% + 14% + 6% + 5% = 30% (approximate total percentage of the other gases in the mixture)
100% – 30% = 70% (percentage of water vapor in the gas mixture)

Chapter Four

Page 19

He can use 22,200 square feet for planting.
74% = 0.74
0.74 x 30,000 square feet =
22,200 square feet
26% of the land and 7,800 square feet are unusable for planting.
100% – 74% = 26%
26% = 0.26
0.26 x 30,000 square feet =
7,800 square feet

Page 21

The area is 104 square miles.
length x width = area
13 miles x 8 miles =
104 square miles

Chapter Five

Page 28

The height of Mount Tambora was reduced by 3,646 feet.
13,000 feet – 9,354 feet =
3,646 feet

GLOSSARY

active (AK-tiv) currently erupting or likely to erupt

caldera volcanoes (kal-DAIR-uh vol-KAY-nose) volcanoes formed by enormous explosions or by the collapse of their central part

cinder cone (SIN-dur KOHN) a small, cone-shaped volcano formed by cinders from an eruption collecting close to the vent

crater (KRAY-tur) a deep hole formed by a collapse or explosion at the vent of a volcano

dormant (DOR-muhnt) not active, but could erupt again

hydrothermal vents (HYE-druh-THUR-muhl VENTS) cracks in the ocean floor that shoot out heated water

igneous rock (IG-nee-uhss) rock produced by a volcano

lava (LAH-vuh) hot, melted rock emitted by a volcano

magma (MAG-muh) the molten rock under Earth's surface that forms igneous rock when it cools

molten (MOHLT-uhn) melted

shield volcanoes (SHEELD vol-KAY-nose) broad, rounded volcanoes that are built up by very fluid lava over time

stratovolcanoes (STRA-toh-vol-KAY-nose) volcanoes made of erupted cinders and ash with occasional lava flows

vent (VENT) the opening of a volcano in Earth's surface

FOR MORE INFORMATION

BOOKS

Rubin, Ken. *Volcanoes & Earthquakes.* New York: Simon & Schuster, 2007.

Stewart, Melissa. *Earthquakes and Volcanoes.* Washington, D.C.: Smithsonian; New York: Collins, 2008.

WEB SITES

FEMA for Kids: Volcanoes
www.fema.gov/kids/volcano.htm
Learn more about volcanoes and how to protect yourself in a disaster

Volcano World's Games and Fun Stuff
volcano.oregonstate.edu/kids/fun/fun.html
Play volcano games and solve volcano puzzles

INDEX

ABOUT THE AUTHOR

John Nestor has been a writer and editor for more than 15 years. He has written about subjects ranging from ducklings hatching in a second grade classroom to Tiger Woods winning The Masters.

John lives in northwest Connecticut with his wife Nancy and their three children James, Jack, and Samantha.